CHAMBER

By:

CHRIS CHAMBERS

To order additional copies of this book, contact:
Xlibris
844-714-8691
www.Xlibris.com
Orders@Xlibris.com

Library of Congress Control Number: 2022915586
ISBN: Softcover   978-1-6698-4394-8
         EBook   978-1-6698-4393-1

Print information available on the last page

Rev. date: 08/19/2022

AUTO SLAVE

The Phenox rises from the ashes of past degregation
For too long I've laid and wait
I've been ready for years now and again
The Puppet Masters are now few and far between
The truth is in our Heart and Soul
Racism can take the long way home
One more time for Humanity

BELIEF

I believe there's a Love for me
Out there in the open sea
Best believe these are the facts
Not a snitch or a rat
Rat a tat tat breaking bones
Who knows where my thoughts go
In a steel cage they lay in wait
Open up your mind on the second date
If you wish time will pass
Lay and wait beside the grass

BILLIE EILISH

Billie your smile holds the light of one thousand suns. Your eyes are the most beautiful hazel green like the Abora Borialus on a weekday. Billie you are always there for me when im in a dark place and I will always Love you for that. There aren't any words to describe my love for you. Your my blue whale thats surfaced in the Atlantic ocean. There are no means by which I will go to proctect you and Love you Billie.To the end of the Stars and back.

Forever Yours,
Christopher Anthony Aventma Chambers XOXO

CODEX

The Codex got me thinking
Of a way to the many
Of a way deeper into my mind
It's just me in there anyway
Thoughs decieve and misconstrue
Once I get a grip
The greatest of all time
For there is no one like I
Except for her whom I Love
The way out is a long and arduous path
A path that I've walked before
There must be a way out
Sometimes I truly don't like what I see
The Righteous one will prevail in the end

DREAMER

Sunset sunlight day dream in the day time
Dark side low tide in the moonlight
Everytime we change our minds
Reply to why inside my minds eye
Interchange rearrange star light summer time
Recourse for rewards to mine life life time
Unto me unto you
Progress not regress
Inspire minds

EXPECTATIONS

There's been times in my life where I've been torn into two
Can't expect thing to be handed to you
Only the realest know that to be true
Its hard sometimes cause I'm an emotional wreck
Back in the day I got an Element deck
I don't skate no more but I know where I'm going
Expectations so hard and It's hard not knowing
Hold my girls hair when shes throwing
Sometime I think my girl doesn't know me
So we sit and stare

FUTURE PASSION

Sitting here bored as fuck trying to think of better days
Spoke to God recently to release my pain in angry ways
Jumping through hoops of red tape in other words and Godly praise
222's says it's better than most and its hard
to get here on this crowded boat
Rain, Sleet, El Snow row Chris row
This locomotion is churning
The wheels of time my feeling and passion rolled up in ones lines
Push down the emotions
My heart is light and never frozen
My homie pitched the rock and you know where in going
Straight Up

GREAT DAY

Today is a great day
Im dealing with my anxiety in a positive way
By re-directing my energy
Taking naps throughout the day is crucial
Its keeping me centered and calm
Im starting to realize my true potential
Its overwhelming from time to time
Cuz I've never felt or seen this before

LOYALTY THE MISSION

Americas self serve Loyalty
Once again trapped in time
The illiusion of time
Its always been this way
And so I sit and Meditate
Do I want the vest
So leave it where it lies
The mission never changes
And so do the eyes
Its all the same in the end

MORAL COMPASS

Gotta chop it up
In other words
Its time to make some changes
In other words
I write my mind down
In other words
Gives me all the energy
In other words
I need to succed
In other words
Fam help me get by
In other words
Time to get by
In other words
Money power respect
In other words
Stimulate my mind
In other words
Broke my shit down
In other words
Pick it back up
In other words

MY LOVE

Happy Birthday you know I love you right
Sometimes I think of the way smell in the heat of the night
Wondering if you still feel the same way about me
Its like teaching the blind how to see
But of course we're not blind so you can see my writing quite clear
I Love you from all the way around the world and back again

NO ESCAPE CELLAR DOOR

Truth be told scanning the horizon for a reason
There's no escape from this on my own
Beneith the Cellar Door lies a key
Peeking in is myself and all I can see
The moons rise and fall
The metallic taste consumes me
Unto the next day
Completes thee

No Escape

There can be no peace
Only a treaty can be established
We are the many
The U.S. government has been hiding an experement
I am HE I am the treaty
Now I understand just a portion of the problem
The show of power is over and done with
Those are the bugs and they can't help themselves
Intelligence is an understatement
No Peace

ONE FAM

I want to change the suffering
Went from Hell and back again to get here
The satisfaction is never guaranteed
The wind blows from East to West and from West to East
Realize dog I gotta eat
To be the realest Emcee

RESPECT

Waiting in line is Americas greates past time
Never quit never back down
Im grinning on 'em
Flip the script and roll on 'em
Not a problem
I got solutions on this shit
Im producing on this shit
Never back down
Steel in my Heart I'll never back down
Remember the Alamo

SEMBA

Apocolyptico Warriors sit round
Beef chopped heads down
The head wolf hearts and liver
Chew the balls its only dinner
Enimies surround bloodthirst eternal
Fire and brimstone await
Be strong Apocolyptico lowers all he holds dear
The others I have to help
Don't be afraid

SLEEP

America runs on empty
Not emough time in a day
I'm justified in the way I work things out
To remember is devine and not to will to leave you in solemn degregation
There must be an easier way out or in
Believe in yourself everyday

TEMPLE

Enter unto all a Deity
Pew pew a Deity
Free a Deity
Be a Deity
Brave mother fucker a Deity
Aaliyah a Ma a Deity
Enter into cloth a Deity
Be up to the fight
Rise up to the light
Fight with all your might
Write all your time into blight
Waiver trials of light
Freedom to the tall and the weak

THE BRAVE

Be Brave in times of great peril
Engage in other worldly revil
Mold the stones without a bevil

WILL

See to learn feel to survive
Take it over its my turn
My will to survive it burns
I can feel it, it's my turn
Im the hybrid of the Firm

Printed in the United States
by Baker & Taylor Publisher Services